FACE PAINTING

Photography
Thomas Heinser
Will Mosgrove
Doug Peck
Kim Raftery

Face Designs
Sarah Tomato
Alice Blandy
Terran Benveniste
Naomi Caspe
Doug Kipping

By the editors of Klutz Press, Palo Alto, California

Dedication

To Cricket Bird, for the inspiration

Acknowledgments

Jester Enterprises
Marilyn Green
Denise Griffith Simons
Elizabeth Root
Sally Peck
Louise Landreth
Terry Konstantine
Shigeo Nakatani
And, of course, all of the kids

Project Coordinator

Kim Gilbert Raftery

Design and Art Direction

Koc•McHenry

Illustration

Sara Boore

Klutz Press
2121 Staunton Court, Palo Alto, CA 94306　　Printed in Singapore.

4 1 5 8 5 7 0 8

Table of Contents

INTRODUCTION

I will start with the only rule in this book. I call it the Prime Commandment to Face Painting. Since it is so important, you must read it carefully and repeat it out loud three times. It's that kind of rule. Here it is. Get ready.

There is no such thing as a mistake in face painting.

It's true. Face painting is that blessed rarity, a zero-mistake activity. Put a red blob on a child's cheek, and you've got an apple. Show them a mirror and they'll love you. Add another green blob, call that a leaf, and you're Picasso. It's incredible. A dream come true for the artistically hopeless.

What makes face painting so uniquely forgiving? How come even you can do it?

I'll be brutally frank. The secret does not lie in your undiscovered talent, much as you might have. The secret is in your "canvas"; you're painting on one of Nature's greatest acts of purest beauty—a child's happy face. When you start that far ahead, it's impossible to blow it.

P.S. As an added bonus, face painting is like giving a foot rub. Your audience is incredibly non-picky. All you have to do is try and you're a star.

4

A Word About the Paints

Our face paints are water-based cosmetics (NOT grease). You can mix and use them as you do any watercolors, but keep them out of direct sun.

The manufacturer of our paints is Kryolan GmbH, the largest, most respected name in theatrical make-up in the world. The Kryolan company is located in West Berlin and has been family-owned for 45 years. Kryolan paints use only ingredients that have been approved as non-toxic cosmetics by the United States Federal Drug Administration as well as every regulatory agency in Western Europe.

Having said that, I should also mention that skin allergies exist to every substance. If any sensitivity to the paints appears, please discontinue their use immediately. If you like, you may use the address in the back of the book, and return it for a full refund.

Equipment

You'll need: a jar of water, a small clean sponge, a big T-shirt or towel to use as a smock, and a volunteer "paintee" with a clean face. Optional equipment would be a few cotton swab Q-tips, and a couple of alcohol towelettes. Q-tips are easier to handle than paintbrushes for kids or ham-handed grown-ups and they work fine for all but the most detailed work. Towelettes make clean-up go faster if you use them before going to the sink. Inexpensive foam rubber cosmetic sponges work a little better than sink sponges, so you might pick up a bag the next time you're at the drug store.

Getting Started

Once you've set out your paints next to a jar of warm water, and then gotten your paintee to pick a design and sit up on the counter, the hardest part is over.

Put a few drops of water into each color pot, just enough to soften the paint, and then moisten the brush in the jar of clean water. Swab a good dose of color onto the brush (don't be stingy), then repeat out loud the Prime Commandment to Face Painting, and start right in. Always keep the brush moist (not drippy) by going frequently to your jar. When you switch colors, rinse the brush out thoroughly so as not to mix.

If you like, you can use Q-tips instead of a brush. They work just about as well for anything but the really detailed designs, and they're easier to handle. Use one per color since they don't rinse out very well.

Our paints take a minute or two to dry, and it makes sense to wait if you're going to be putting two colors right next to one another.

Ask your paintee to keep as still as possible so as to avoid the paint-in-ear problem. And, in the same vein, don't talk to them while you're en route. In order to minimize the jitters, plant a pinky down somewhere on their face to anchor your painting hand.

A Word About the Eyes

As you'll soon see, a lot of the designs on the following pages involve putting paint up close to the eyes. Naturally, this is optional. If you don't feel comfortable working close to anyone's eyes, all the designs work fine with the paint kept away from the eyes too.

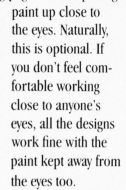

If you do choose to use the paints around the eyes, as we have, use the same kind of caution as you would in applying any kind of eye make-up—a steady hand with no poking and no jabbing. And no glitter in the eye area, because of the chance of irritation.

One final caution: While all of the European and Japanese regulatory agencies have approved it, the FDA recommends that the red color be kept away from the immediate eye area as well.

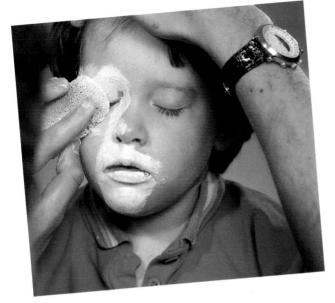

Applying Whiteface

A number of the designs that follow, particularly some of the clown faces, use a white base to build upon. You can skip it or not, as you wish. Alternatively, you can put a whiteface base behind many designs here that don't show them. It all depends. In our experience, kids love whiteface because it's a little extreme. As one of our volunteer paintees so aptly put it: "Some is good, and more is better, but maximum is the best."

The technique is simple. Use a damp but not drippy sponge and swab it around in the white pot. Don't be shy, you should load it up pretty well. Then ask your volunteer to close their eyes gently—no squinting—and relax their face ("Pretend you're sleeping"). Start with the sponge at the top of the forehead and sweep around along the side of the face in one long stroke to the point of the chin. Use long gentle strokes and work your way into the center of the face. We go right over the closed eyes, but you can do as you choose.

It's generally not necessary to double-coat, as that often creates a streaky look, but you may well have to re-dampen the sponge and go back to the pot before you finish the whole face.

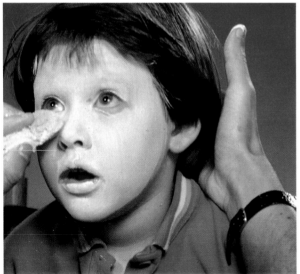

Let it dry for a couple of minutes before starting in with the overlaying colors.

Clean-up

Kryolan paints are watercolors, which means they will wash off skin with only soap and water—although a pre-scrubbing with alcohol towelettes can help.

When the paints get smeared on clothes, they'll wash off as easily as any watercolor, which is to say—it can be a little tricky, particularly with the red pigment. As always, if you wipe any mess off before it fully dries (in this case, that takes only a minute or two), you'll have better luck. The best idea is to wear clothing that's been Mom-approved for watercoloring activities, or to use a smock or apron.

Mixing and Matching

If you want to mix colors, you can do that in a separate, clean little dish. Or, even easier, you can do it in the pots themselves. If you want orange, for example, just mix a little yellow right into the red pot. When you're done, wipe off the orange top layer with a sponge, and you're back to red again. Simple.

Razzle Dazzle, Bells and Whistles, Glitter and Sequins

As one veteran face painter told us, no matter how blobby-looking your design turns out, you can always save it with glitter. Buy <u>fine</u> or <u>superfine</u> glitter from your crafts store. Regular artwork glitter is too abrasive on the skin. Stay clear of the eyes, and apply it with a damp fingertip right onto the paint when it's still wet.

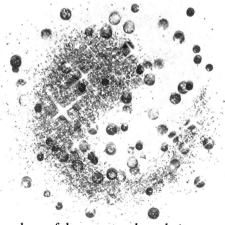

Color Cookbook:

ORANGE = YELLOW
+ RED

PINK = WHITE
+ RED

PURPLE = BLUE
+ RED

BROWN = BLACK
+ RED

Glitter isn't recommended for young children, who might rub their faces and get it into their eyes.

Sequins are another trick of the trade. Use just a tiny dab of eyelash adhesive (from the drugstore), or make up a little bit of your own (a drop each of Elmer's + water + hand lotion). Stay clear of the eyes, and apply tastefully, as always.

As a last resort, if your cupboard is otherwise bare, bring out the stickers and stick away (being careful not to get them tangled in any hair).

Kid-to-Kid Face Painting

Parents should not neglect this all-important, and highly attractive, dimension to face painting. Depending on age, kid-to-kid face painting can work very well with a bare minimum of supervision. For younger kids, I'd recommend Q-tips or just plain fingers instead of the brush. Less chance of getting poked. As far as subject matter, for the younger set, Indian war paint, or some simple geometric pattern works fine. Older kids can set their sights as high as they like. See particularly the feet painting in the Body Art section. And to lengthen the activity enough to fill up a whole rainy afternoon, set out materials for appropriate costume construction.

Birthday Parties

Face painting was practically invented for parties, fairs and fundraisers. It's one of the few activities absolutely guaranteed to be a winner. With the help of this book, and the parent's normal quota of blind confidence, you need never fear another birthday party again in your life.

One caution: If you're going to be doing face painting at a party at all, you should realize that nearly everyone there will want it. As a result, a party face painter has to be prepared for volume.

"Volume" in face painting means cheek art. It's the only kind that can be done in a minute or two. Unless you've got the time or assistance to take on the bigger projects, flip the book open to the cheek art section and keep it there.

Set up a little corner where you have a paintee's stool, a chair and an area to work in. Bring out a supply of tissues or alcohol towelettes, a box of Q-tips (optional) and a towel or smock. When you've decided the time is ripe, hang out your sign and get ready for your very first customer. (Your very first customer, incidentally, is a crucial one because of the fact that most kids will want whatever the kid in front of them got. You might think hard about that if Customer Number One wants a full-face Count Drac.)

Cheek art is an especially popular kind of face painting at birthday parties and school fairs where speed counts. In addition, when you're dealing with older kids who have, regrettably, reached the "age of self consciousness," cheek art is the safest kind of face painting. Amongst adults, almost all of whom are hopelessly self-conscious, cheek art is frequently the only way to go. (Having said that, it should definitely be noted that for women, a discreet little flower on the upper cheek, with a touch of glitter, can be downright glamorous if you do it right.) The roots of cheek art are, of course, tied in with roots of cosmetics in general—and those are roots that go back as far as you care to look. In traditional Chinese opera, for example, performers wear "masks" that are actually created with nothing but facepaints.

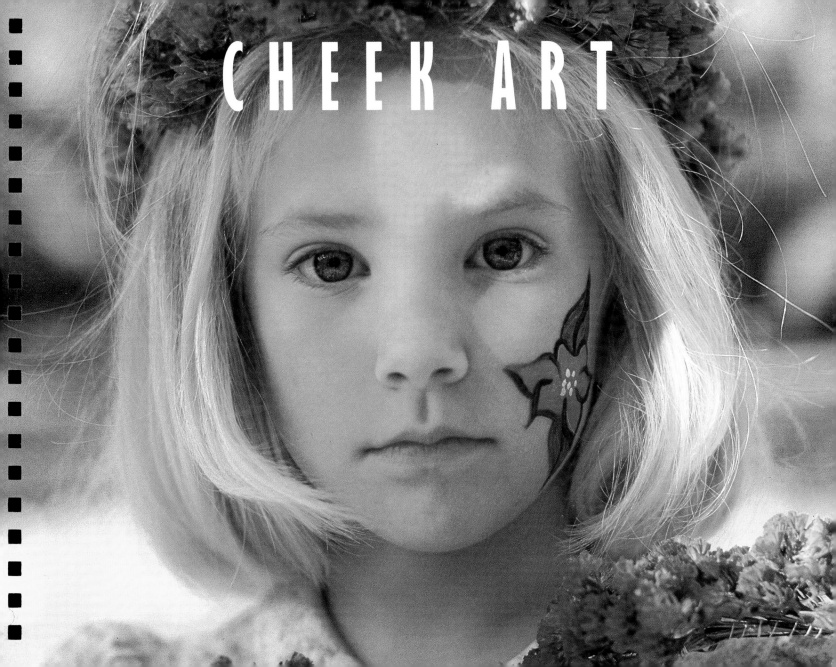

CHEEK ART

Hearts and Rainbows

Hearts and Rainbows are frequently the Number One favorite motif at big and little girl birthday parties. In addition to what is shown here, of course, you can put hearts on toenails, fingernails, noses, etc.

16

A snowman for the holidays ● A dolphin cheek for marine mammal fans ● A striped warrior face
● An ice cream cheek (two scoops on a sugar cone) ● Flamingoes are always in style ● A dinosaur
cheek for fans of the Mesozoic Period

Dragon

An Apache shield cheek out of the Old West ● Dinosaur #2 (but this one's a plant eater) ● Teddy bear, an all-time classic ● A blue daisy cheek ● Unicorns are another very popular cheek design ● A pumpkin for Halloween

Saturn

Part of the Flash Gordon look popular throughout the galaxy.

20

Five-legged Octopus

A rare, miniature cousin to the more common oversized eight-legged octopus, ours lives in sidewalk puddles rather than oceans and is always eager to make friends with anyone as big as we are.

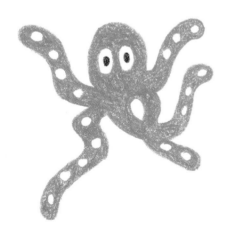

Storms, Stars and Cherries

When you paint yourself up to look like the family hound, or a friendly lion, or a spotless leopard, you're adding your own link to a chain that goes back a very, very long way. Back to when men and animals lived side by side, often running after the same thing for dinner. At that time, humans must have envied the animals their speed and hunting abilities—and primitive men often dressed themselves as animals in an effort to pick up some of their strength and spirit. Today, animals still hold the same basic attraction for people, despite the fact that we usually don't fight over meals anymore. The following face designs came out of the family feeling that we have for animals and have probably been popular, in one form or another, for about 50,000 years.

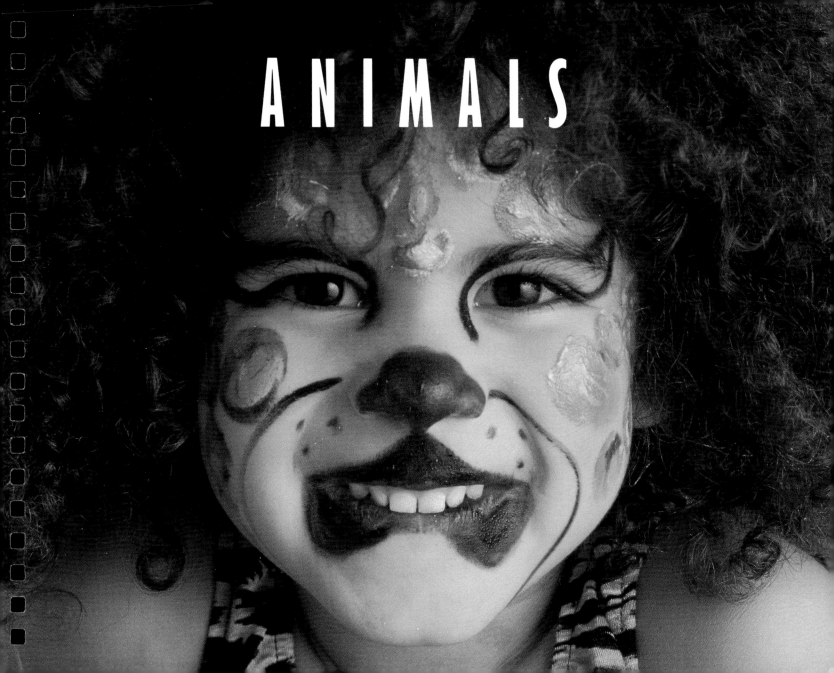

ANIMALS

The whiteface base (see p. 8) is particularly optional here.

El Dog

If you've been thinking about getting a dog, but have been worried about the expense and responsibility, here's a chance to take the idea on a test drive. When you're done painting, get a stick and head for the front yard.

1. Create brown by mixing the red and the black, and apply spots with your fingertip as shown.

2. Black goes on last. Don't forget the whisker holes, since they help a lot to make the face "doggy."

27

1. Mix yellow and red together to make your orange, and use it to make about 12 stripes (imagine a clock face starting at the chin). **2.** To add the yellow stripes, just fill in between the orange. Also use the yellow under the eyes. **3.** Add the black stripes by painting over half the yellow stripes. **4.** Add the white. **5.** Go back to your black. Outline the area under the nose, add the whisker holes, and then blob some onto the end of the nose.

Stripey Tiger

House Mouse

1. Apply a full whiteface (see p. 8). Still using the sponge, dab on a faint pink rouge at the cheekbones. Create pink by mixing red and white and find the cheekbones by asking your paintee to suck in their cheeks.

3. Add the black eyebrows, whiskers, nose, etc.

2. Using your brush, frame the whole face in black. Start by shaping the three points, at the top and on the sides. By keeping your eye on the bridge of the nose, you keep the symmetry. Once the points are in place, use long continuous strokes to join them.

4. Ask your paintee to pucker up, then apply the ruby red lips with a fingertip. You might want to use a brush around the edges.

Whisker Cat

1.
Pick a favorite color and load your brush up.

2.
Draw the whisker and mouth lines.

3.
Eyes should always be relaxed and closed when you paint near them.

4.
The ears are construction paper triangles taped to a hairband.

Leopard Loud

1. Sponge on a full yellow face starting at the peak of the forehead and sweeping around the side of the face in one long stroke to the point of the chin. Still using strokes as long as possible, work across the face, skipping the eyes, the nose and the area above the mouth.

2. Use your brush to fill in with white the area above the mouth.

3. Again with the brush, paint in all the black: the eyebrows, the whiskers and the three semi-circles on each cheek.

4. For a final touch, mix up a little yellow and red, then underline the eyebrows, smear some onto the nose and dab a little into the semicircles.

Zebra

This is one of the more dramatic faces. Very popular with zoo-goers and fans of East African wild animals and, because of its exact symmetry, easy to do.

1. Start with a sponged-on, full whiteface base (see introduction). Wait a couple of minutes for it to dry.

2. Apply the black lines as illustrated, keeping in mind two things: One, the left side of the face is identical to the right; and two, don't be nervous or hesitant. Load your brush up fully and go for long, confident strokes.

Big Paws

Big Paws has a face practically identical to our howling white-face hound on page 27 except you can hold the white.

Grocery Bag Big Feet

1. Ingredients: Five grocery bags, a bunch of newspaper, tape and a magic marker.

2. Stuff two bags with crumpled up newspaper. To keep the newspaper from coming out the open tops, pull another grocery bag over each of them. Tape them together.

3. Cut holes to stick your feet into and try on for size. To make toes, cut them out from the extra grocery bag and tape them on. Don't forget to paint your paper toenails with the magic marker.

Wildcat

Our Wildcat is a member of the *felinicus deviticus* family (Latin for "animal who destroys furniture"). As a result, he or she is best kept outdoors. In addition, they prefer to dress in leotards or tights with a bathrobe belt tail.

1. The most important feature of this face is the black around the nose and mouth and the whisker holes, so get out your brush and start there. Before you put away the black, outline the eyes (while they're relaxed and closed).

2. Since your cat is wild, the rest of the face is fairly free-form. Use your fingertip to splotch on yellow and orange around the cheeks and above the eyes. (Orange = yellow + red).

3. Finish up with black again, dabbing it with the brush in a couple of squiggles around the color splotches.

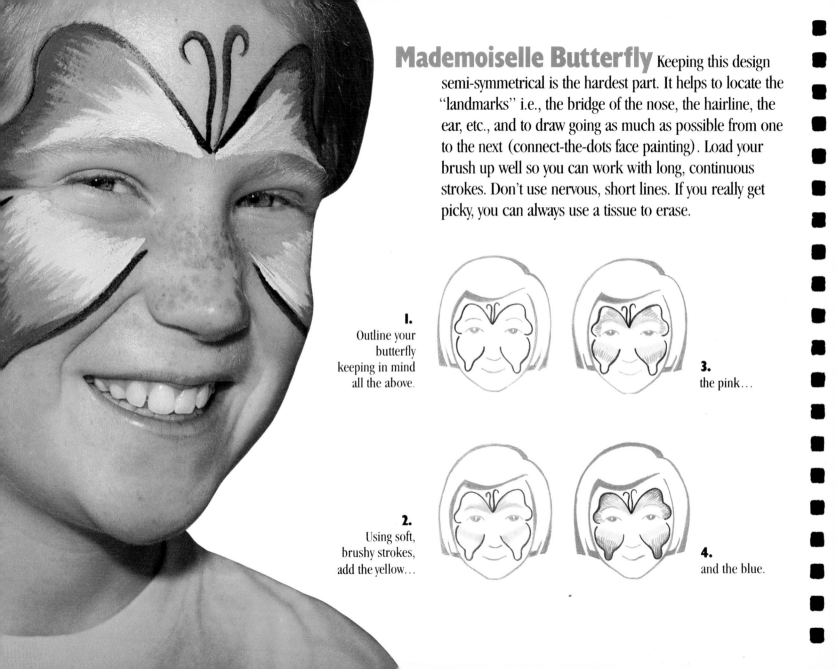

Mademoiselle Butterfly

Keeping this design semi-symmetrical is the hardest part. It helps to locate the "landmarks" i.e., the bridge of the nose, the hairline, the ear, etc., and to draw going as much as possible from one to the next (connect-the-dots face painting). Load your brush up well so you can work with long, continuous strokes. Don't use nervous, short lines. If you really get picky, you can always use a tissue to erase.

1.
Outline your butterfly keeping in mind all the above.

2.
Using soft, brushy strokes, add the yellow…

3.
the pink…

4.
and the blue.

Two-Tooth Rabbit

Two-tooth can be done with or without the black eyes, although, on the "more is better" theory, most kids like them.

I. Do the cotton cheeks in white with your fingertip; use the brush (or Q-tip) around the edges. Paint in the teeth with your brush.

2. Add the eye-patches (optional) in black, and outline the cheeks and teeth.

3. Finally, in black, add the whiskers, whisker holes and, of course, a pink nose (mix up your white and red).

Cotton Ears

Ingredients: A bag of cotton balls, Elmer's, a stapler, felt tip pens and construction paper. Cut out all the pieces, color in appropriately, then glue the cotton for the furry ear look. For a better fit, put the headband on first for size, then hold the two ends together while you take it off to staple it.

37

Human beings have a basic need to get goofy. It's genetic and comes from the silly gland, an important organ located in the little toe. When yours starts to act up, you shouldn't fight it. A lot of people do and all they get are headaches and a burning sensation in their tummies. The following faces are meant for absolutely nothing but being silly and horsing around. When you paint one of them on, you'll become part of a tradition that reaches back through more than a thousand years, linking you to the court jesters of Renaissance Europe, ancient Rome and Egypt. In those days, the "jester" was a very special character, the only one who could do and say exactly as he pleased around the king. Even today, when you put your clown face on, you'll find you can get away with a little more than usual.

CLOWNS

mppety Almost always wears rolled up pants, suspenders and a loud tie. Has a fondness for way-too-big hats or wigs. Can never find both shoes but knows how to make do with buckets instead by taping his feet to the inside of them with grey duct tape.

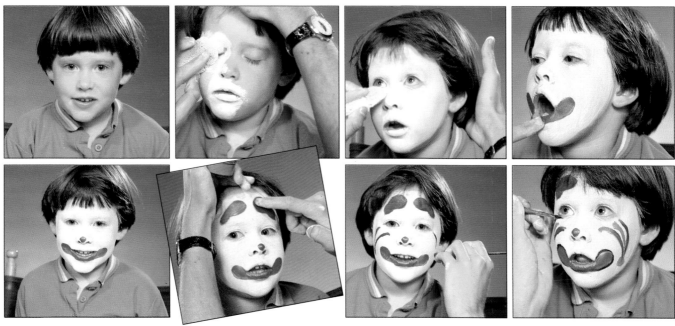

1. Start with a likely looking suspect. **2.** Begin by sponge-applying a whiteface base (see introduction for a full description of how). **3.** We do full careful paint around the eyes, but it's always your option. **4.** Fingers work well for applying clown mouths. **5.** The black outline on the mouth is optional, but if done, it's best to do it after the red. **6.** Steady the head to minimize jitters, and use your finger for big blobby shapes. **7.** Use the brush for all the line work… **8.** …and final details.

Lady Bigshirt

Likes to get into Dad's stuff and wears his shirts with a crepe paper flower or just a loud tie. Also knows how to make a collar out of a piece of string plus ruffled fabric or stiff crinkly paper.

I. Start with a full sponge-applied whiteface base (see p. 8 for full instructions).

3. The yellow teardrops are next. Outline them in black if you like.

2. The red nose and mouth can best be applied with a fingertip and "finalized" with a brush. Same as the blue eyebrows.

4. The red teardrop and orange flourishes at the corners of the eyes are the finishing touches. As always, wait a minute or two before putting two colors next to one another.

Bright Eyes

Bright eyes is more of an old-fashioned court jester than a modern clown. To create his face, start with the white paint and make use of "landmarks" on the face to help with the symmetry. For example, the white curls start at the point of the chin, and follow the chin line to an imaginary line drawn straight down from the end of the eyebrow. As always, wait a minute or two until the paint dries before you apply another color right next to it.

Sequins and Glitter

These are the razzle dazzle of face painting. No matter how sloppy your paint is, glitter will make it a work of art. The introduction has a fuller description of how and where to apply glitter and sequins, but, in brief, here are the key points: Use eyelash adhesive (from the drug store) for the sequins, but the glitter goes on just by sticking against the wet paint. And always, be very careful not to get either the glitter or the sequins near the eyes.

43

Brigadier Bigtooth

Talks very little but loves to make loud noises and can sound exactly like the neighbor's dog if asked. Sometimes carries around a big rubber plumber's helper instead of a cane. Wears beanies, baseball caps or sometimes a small sauce pan.

1. Start with a full sponge-applied white-face base (the introduction has complete instructions).

2. Using your fingertip and brush, add the red around the mouth, eyebrows and nose.

3. While the red is drying, do some free-form cheek splotches.

4. In black, outline the mouth and teeth, and, if you like, add a bit of eyeliner as flourish.

P.S. Our Brigadier has glitter on his nose and eyebrows. If you choose to use it, be careful around the eyes.

44

Frozenpants and Filldastern

A couple of clowns with a lot of energy. They like to wear each other's clothes, sometimes backwards, or even upside down (legs through the sleeves)

1.

2.

3.

4.

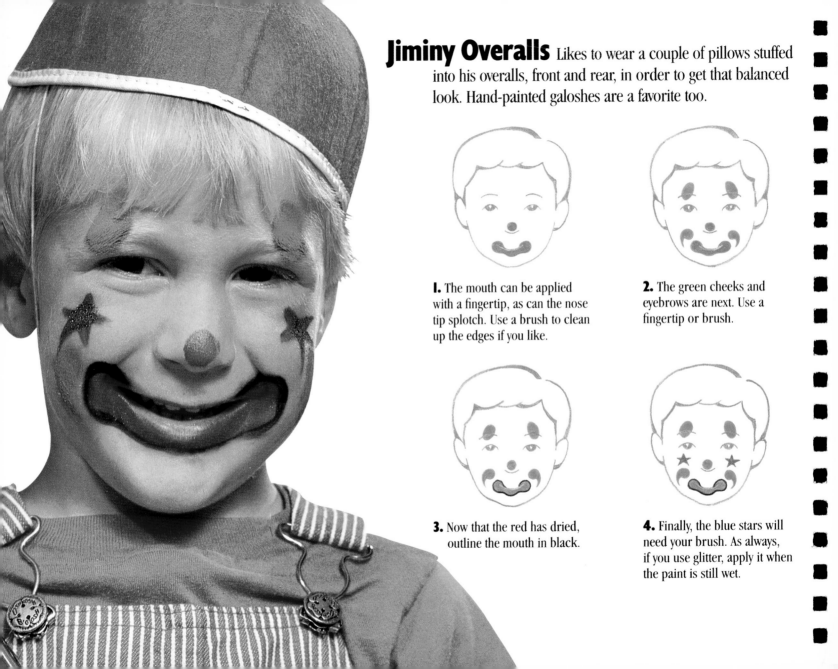

Jiminy Overalls
Likes to wear a couple of pillows stuffed into his overalls, front and rear, in order to get that balanced look. Hand-painted galoshes are a favorite too.

1. The mouth can be applied with a fingertip, as can the nose tip splotch. Use a brush to clean up the edges if you like.

2. The green cheeks and eyebrows are next. Use a fingertip or brush.

3. Now that the red has dried, outline the mouth in black.

4. Finally, the blue stars will need your brush. As always, if you use glitter, apply it when the paint is still wet.

Big Pants

A closet clown (in other words, his costume comes out of his parents' closet). Everything has to be at least 5 sizes too big or it won't fit. The face is a combination of green cheek triangles, a red nose, and a mouth like Lady Bigshirt's. (p. 42)

Getting all dressed up to look like skeletons, witches, monsters, movie stars and various other horrible things, and then trooping around demanding bribes from the neighbors, is a tradition that dates back to the ancient inhabitants of Ireland and the British Isles. It all began more than 2,000 years ago (long before Christmas was first celebrated), and was timed to coincide with the changing of the seasons and the harvesting of the crops. For people who live off the land, it was end of their year. ❧ Originally, it was believed that all the spirits who had died in the previous year rose up on this last day and wandered about, going door-to-door, having one last fling before moving to the Otherworld. In order to keep these spirits happy (and out of the house), food and drink were left for them on the doorstep.

HALLOWEEN

Coverghoul has received a full white-face base (see introduction for a complete set of instructions). After it dried, he got a sponge treatment with the pale green and black around the eyes and sunken cheeks. The fangs were a last minute addition. Most important, of course, was the alarming hairdo. We got that by putting a good dose of white face paint on our fingers and running them through his hair, more or less like hair mousse.

...a the Friendly ...st

A simple, but scary spook. The whiteface base is applied first (see p. 8). Black or blue is lightly sponge-applied around the hollow eyes. Don't forget the safety pin under the chin (plus a discreet hairband) to keep the sheet in place.

The Accident Victim

"Help stamp out faulty elevators!"

Wrap a head bandage on the victim first, before any paint. We used a box or two of gauze, but a torn up old sheet works nearly as well.

1. Start with a complete whiteface base (see the introduction for a full set of instructions). Add some black bags under the eyes after the base dries.

2. Then bring out the sponge and begin splotching colors on the cheeks and eyes. Use green, blue, and mix up some brown for that gravel-burn look.

3. Create some reddish brown (red + black) for dried blood, and sponge it on delicately here and there. Don't forget to get it up onto the head bandage where it can ooze out between the gauze.

Frankenstein

I. Start with a splotchily applied whiteface base (see p. 8 for full instructions). After it dries add the hollow eyes by sponging on a blue-black mix.

2. With your sponge, apply a seasick green here and there.

3. The scars and stitches are black, and, as always, let your own good taste be your guide as to where and how many.

A size 44 long Goodwill brand suit coat, with modified shoe boxes as shoulder pads, was all we used for wardrobe.

51

The Princess

1. Start with full whiteface. Then, starting with a fingertip and finishing with a brush, add pink cheek blush and lips.

2. Add red and blue stars (use your brush) after the blush has dried. Then, with your fingertip, add a little eyeshadow.

3. You can add eyebrows and a black line from the corners of the eyes for mystery.

Count Drac and the Princess

The Count gets out mostly at night and as a result likes to dress in basic black. The critical thing of course is the cape. A dark sports coat—about 5 sizes too big—with safety pins at the neck will work in a pinch. But a real cape, made with a square of dark fabric, hemmed and tied with a piece of yarn is a vampire's dream. ✰ The Princess goes in for the June bride look. A half-slip will work as her veil and a plastic headband decorated with ribbons and frillies makes a nice tiara.

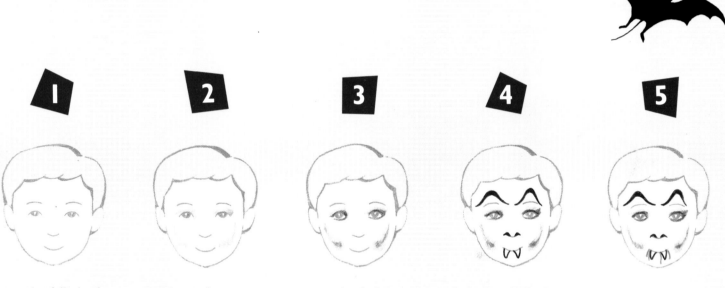

1	2	3	4	5
Start with a full whiteface (introduction has complete instructions).	With your fingertip or sponge, apply a pale purple (red + blue) "shadow" to the cheekbones and eyelids. Ask your volunteer to suck in his or her cheeks to help you find their cheekbones.	Deepen the shadows just a bit with your fingertip and some black.	Then, using the brush draw in arching eyebrows, fangs and nostrils.	Drool a little red out of the mouth and you're all set.

Ninja Warrior

A fierce face from the Far East that uses a collection of red, white and black stripes for the full, ferocious effect. Put them on (1) red, (2) black and (3) white, allowing time for adjacent or overlapping colors to dry (a minute or two). The most important trick is the same as always: load your brush up well, and use full, confident strokes. Don't try dabbing the lines together with timid little strokes.

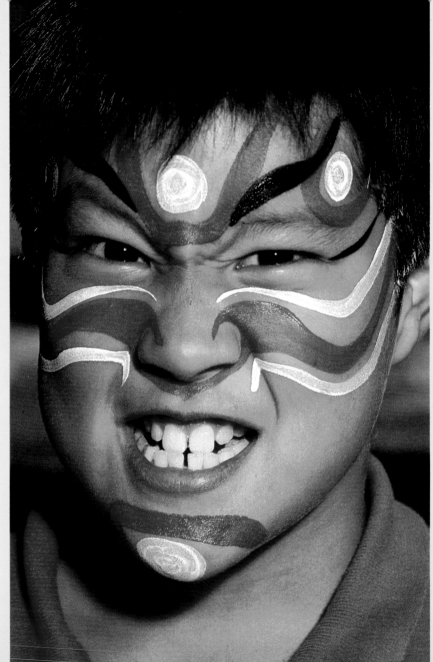

1.

2.

3.

Glinda
the Usually Good Witch of the North

1. Start with a pale, sponged on, "seasick green."

2. Add the eyebrows and warts.

3. Using your fingertip add the ruby lips.

4. Finally, a light blue eye shadow for glamorous witches.

● The Three Grunps

This is the perfect opportunity to apply the paints like make-up. Mix red and white for pink blush, and blue and white for eyeshadow. Use your sponge to apply them both, then use your brush to draw in the hornrims and moustache. Dab on a beauty spot and don't be shy with the ruby lips. Apply the red with your fingertip and add detail with the brush. Raid the attic for the rest of the costume and call the limo.

Captain Cutthroat

Although we didn't paint one ourselves, a livid scar can look very nice on the captain. Our own saber came out of the toy box, but you can easily substitute a homemade hook. Roll some tinfoil into the appropriate shape and poke one end of it through a paper cup.

1. Mix up a little grey (black + white) and apply it like 5 o'clock shadow.

2. Use black and the brush for the eyepatch and moustache.

57

One of the most distinctive things about human beings is that, unlike most animals, they don't seem to like the way they look. Ever since we first swung out of the trees, we've been struggling to improve upon nature. ✔ Back in the woolly mammoth days, that meant wearing animal furs, feathers or bones in the appropriate style. In ages afterward, tattooing became a highly evolved folk art that probably reached its pinnacle in the South Seas (where sailors picked up a taste for it). ✔ Today, we tend to use clothing, jewelry and cosmetics for the same purpose. But one fad has never faded. In virtually every culture, in virtually every time, people have put paint, make-up or dye on themselves, always trying to dress up that just-plain-skin look that we've all been born with.

BODY ART

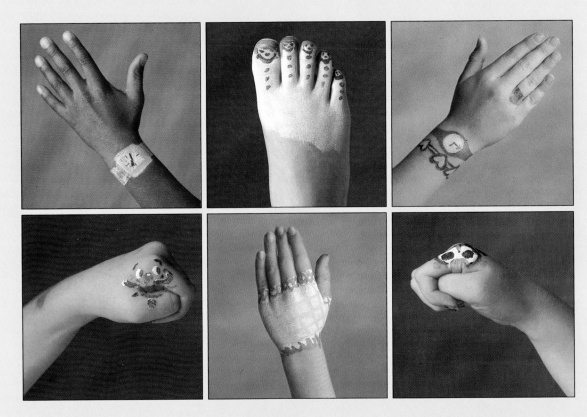

● The watch for people who don't mind being a little late ● Toe People; Mom, Dad and the three little piggies ● More bracelets, watches and rings ● Knuckle Head Number One, work your thumb up and down to make him talk ● Rock 'n Roll glove ● Knuckle Head Number Two, so Knuckle Number One has someone to talk to

Dancing
Knee to Knee

This is a kind of body
language, a chance to
let your knees finally
get to know one
another.

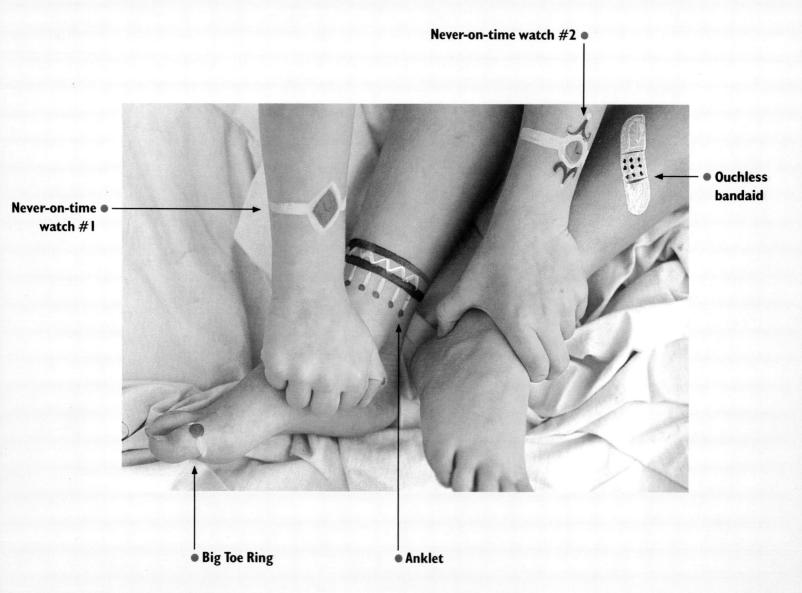

Never-on-time watch #2

Never-on-time watch #1

Ouchless bandaid

Big Toe Ring

Anklet

Hand Painting
When the younger kids want to get in on the action, but are afraid of anything on their face, paint a small design on their wrist or hands. A perfect compromise.

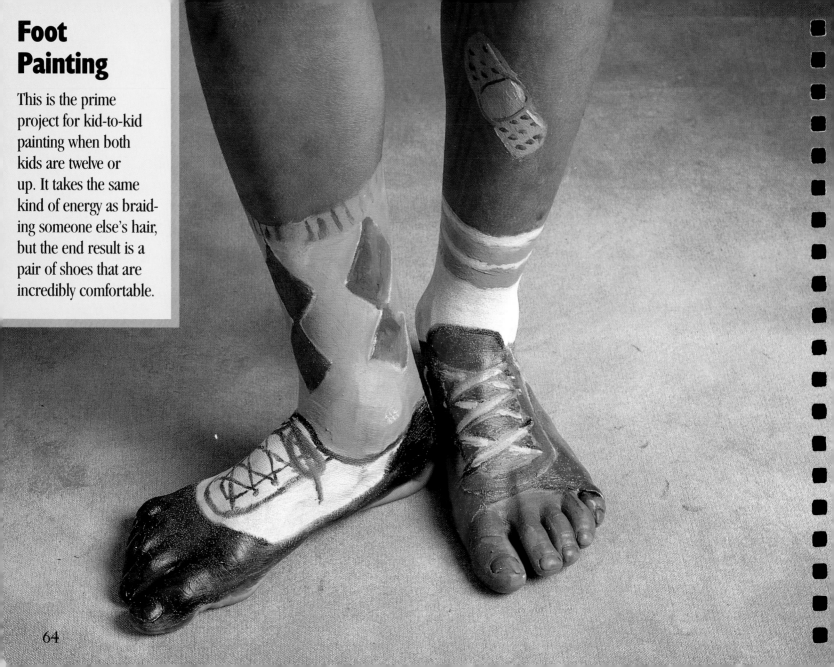

Foot Painting

This is the prime project for kid-to-kid painting when both kids are twelve or up. It takes the same kind of energy as braiding someone else's hair, but the end result is a pair of shoes that are incredibly comfortable.

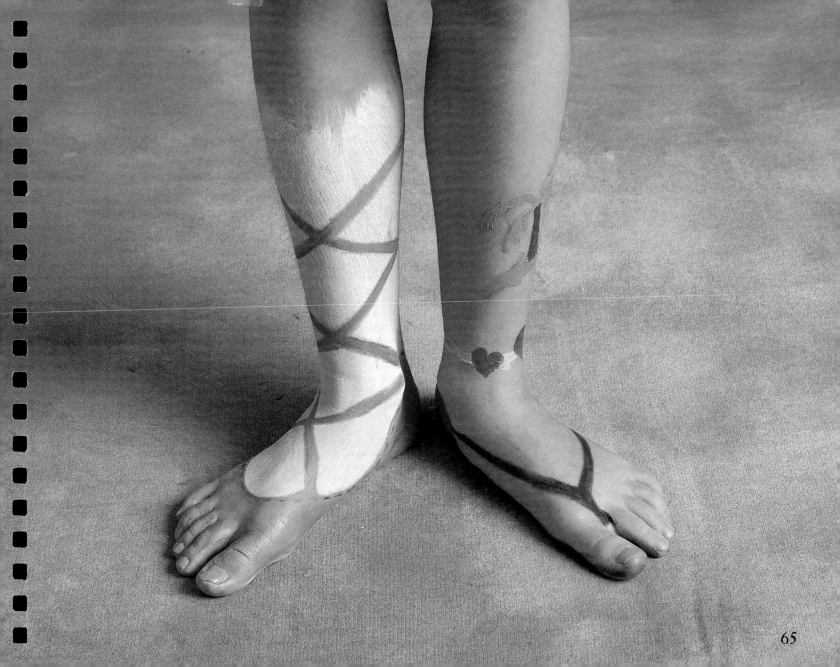

The Kids' Credits Page

The following children lent us their happy faces to appear in our book. We'd like to thank them one and all by name.

Michael Zappert, Russell Young, Keri Yen, Jonathan Wong, Andrew Wollenberg, Joel Weber, Tait Waterman, Athena von Oech, Dinaz Vilms, Kurt Tenenbaum, Gina Taylor, Lanli Szeto, Frida Suro, Casey Strum, Tyler Soper, Ben Soper, Kristine Simons, Jane Roberts, Adam Reininger, Sandrella Plotner, Donald Pipkin, Robert Peck, Ryen Peck, Colin Peck, Maren Pearson, Laura Pearson, Bradley Pearson, Emma McKeithen, Vanessa McCroskey, Kadia Usmano Martin, Knengi Usmano Martin, Sarah Lim, Elliot Lim, Jamie Lenington, Misha Leatherman, Ashleigh Leatherman, John Kraiss, Michele Kraiss, Shiyan Koh, Christopher Judge, Nell Johnson, Brandon Iki, Alice Hunt, Robin Hindery, Wesley Hibbs, Elliot Hibbs, Arabella Hibbs, Bridget Geibel, Lisa Friedrichs, Rena Favstritsky, Lisa Favstritsky, Jamie Dodds, Greg Dodds, Emily Dirks, Wendy Dey, Lauren Dey, Katherine Dey, Cody Cassidy, Robbie Burmeister, Allison Burmeister, Kenneth Bryant, Clint Bradford, Zachary Appelman, Jesse Appelman

The Klutz Flying Apparatus Catalogue

Additional copies of this book, replacement paints, as well as the entire library of Klutz books, are all available in our mail order catalogue. It's available free for the asking.

Klutz Press ● 2121 Staunton Court, Palo Alto, CA 94306 ● (415) 424-0739